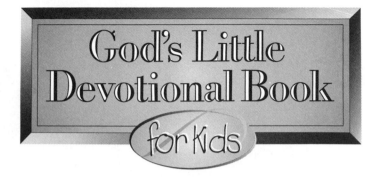

God's Little Devotional Book

for Kids

by
Dr. V. Gilbert Beers

ILLUSTRATIONS BY
JULIE SAWYER

HONOR **HB** BOOKS

An Imprint of Cook Communications Ministries • Colorado Springs, CO

All Scripture quotations are taken from the *International Children's Bible, New Century Version.* Copyright © 1986, 1988 by Word Publishing, Dallas, Texas 75039. Used by permission.

God's Little Devotional Book for Kids
ISBN 1-56292-478-8

11 10 9 8 7 6 5 4 3 2 Printing/Year 07 06 05 04 03

Copyright © 1997, 2001 by Dr. V. Gilbert Beers
P. O. Box 650
Glen Ellyn, Illinois 60138

Published by Honor Books
An Imprint of Cook Communications Ministries
4050 Lee Vance View
Colorado Springs, CO 80918

Designed by Koechel Peterson and Associates, Minneapolis, MN.

Introduction

God has lots of great ideas about how we are to live, how we are to love, and how we are to give. This little book will help you grow and know God's ways, if you follow what it says and live it day by day.

A NOTE TO PARENTS:

God's Little Devotional Book for Kids is based upon the #1 best-seller *God's Little Instruction Book for Kids*. It has been written and designed for children, and includes quotes, rhymes, and bits of wisdom that kids will cherish. Each quote has a scripture verse which unlocks the true meaning of the principle behind the quote. Also included are short stories or prayers that make the scripture come alive for children.

Read the quotes, the scriptures, and the stories to your child, and ask them if they understand. If they don't, explain it to them in your own words. Show them how God's Word is relevant in today's society. And don't be embarrassed if you, yourself, enjoy reading *God's Little Devotional Book for Kids* — it was meant to be treasured and enjoyed by anyone young at heart!

*God accepts anyone
who worships Him
and does what is right.*

ACTS 10:35

Red and yellow,
Black and white,
All are precious,
In God's sight.

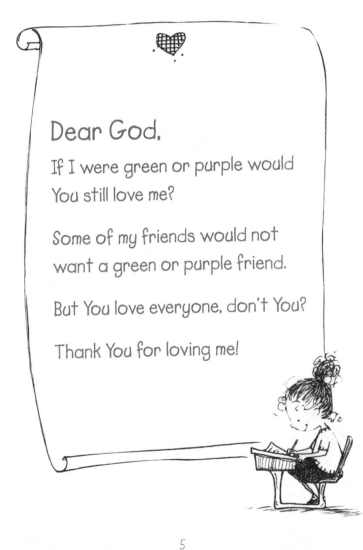

Dear God,

If I were green or purple would You still love me?

Some of my friends would not want a green or purple friend.

But You love everyone, don't You?

Thank You for loving me!

*The Lord God put the man
in the garden of Eden
to care for it and work it.*

GENESIS 2:15

Take care of the earth
For all it's worth!
In all of space,
it's the only place
That's fit for the
human race.

Dear God,

You must really love the earth to make it so beautiful. How do You keep it fixed and running so well? That shows how much You love it, too.

But most of all, You gave this beautiful earth to me and my friends. Help me take care of it the way You would. That will show You how much I love You and Your wonderful gifts.

THE RIGHT TIME

When is the right time to pray?

ALWAYS

When is the right time to play?

SOMETIMES

*When is the right time
to disobey God?*

NEVER

*When is the right time
to read God's Word?*

ALWAYS

*When is the right time
to help our parents?*

WHEN THEY NEED YOU

When is the right time
to make them sad?

NEVER

When is the right time
to love others?

ALWAYS

When is the right time
to love our parents?

ALWAYS

When is the right time
to love God?

ALWAYS

The "right time" is now.

2 CORINTHIANS 6:2

Joy Seeds

One day our family decided to plant a garden.

Dad dug.

Mom raked.

And I watched . . . well, I helped a little.

Mom brought the seed packets from the house.

Dad made little rows for the seeds. Then Dad picked up a little package. It had a picture of carrots on it.

"Let's put these apple seeds in this row," Dad said. "Then we can watch the carrots grow."

I laughed. "Funny, Dad," I said. "Those are carrot seeds. Carrots grow from carrot seeds."

Dad laughed, too. Then he planted the carrot seeds.

Mom picked up another little package. It had a picture of radishes on it.

"Let's put these strawberry seeds in this row," Mom said. "Then we can watch the radishes grow."

I laughed. "Funny, Mom," I said. "Those are radish seeds. Radishes grow from radish seeds."

Mom laughed, too. Then she planted the radish seeds.

Dad picked up another little package.
It looked like an envelope. It did not have
a picture on it.

"Let's plant these seeds," he said.

"What are they?" I asked.

"Joy seeds," said Dad. "They grow joy."

"How do they do that?" I asked.

13

Dad took a little piece of paper from the envelope.

"Help Mom with the dishes," he read. "That would bring joy to Mom."

Then he took another piece of paper from the envelope.

"Tell Dad you love him," he read. "That would bring joy to Dad."

I laughed. "Any more?" I asked.

"Lots," said Dad. "But we'll plant just one more."

Dad took another piece of paper out. "Read your Bible and say your prayers," he read. "That will bring joy to Jesus."

"I would like to plant some of those seeds," I said.

So I did! Would you like to plant some joy seeds, too?

A person harvests
only what he plants.

GALATIANS 6:7

The Father has loved us so much!
He loved us so much that we are called
children of God.

1 JOHN 3:1

God loves you.

*Love has a way
of not looking
at others' sins.*

I PETER 4:8

Dear God,

Is the Bible Your great big
valentine to me?

Thanks for loving me even when
I'm not very loveable.

Thanks for loving me, even if
I don't love You.

Thanks for loving me, every
minute of every day.

Please help me love You
the way You love me.

FORGETTING AND FORGIVING

If you think that you are better

Than Janie, Joe, or Pete,

If you think the things that you have done

Are really pretty neat,

If you think the sins of others

Are darker than your own,

If you think your secret sins

Will never be known,

Then try to look through God's eyes

At each and every one,

Forgiving and forgetting all our sins

When we follow His dear Son.

SATAN SAYS . . .

sin is in so let's begin;

sin is fun for everyone;

wrong is right,

and right is wrong.

so if you're "in" you will belong.

A friend may say . . .

this is in

so let's begin;

this is fun

for everyone;

this is right,

and that is wrong;

so if you're "in"

you will belong.

Jesus ♥ Me

When Wrong Seems Right
and Right Seems Wrong
Be careful! Your friend may be
talking for someone else!

Everyone else can be wrong, but when God is with you, you will be right. Ask Him to be with you now and always.

Sin is what the serpent says is "in."
You must not do wrong
just because everyone else is doing it.

EXODUS 23:2

You're Beautiful!

"**I** wish I were beautiful like other kids," I said to my Sunday school teacher.

"Beauty is not a pretty face or a handsome face," he said. "You're beautiful when you do special things that God wants you to do."

The next day I saw Mom working in the kitchen. She was ironing my clothes and getting dinner for us. Baby was crying.

Something was running over on the stove. She didn't have lipstick on and her hair was a little messy.

"You're beautiful, Mom," I said.

I wasn't sure if Mom would laugh or cry. "You're funny," she said. "Look at me!"

"But you're doing special things that God wants you to do," I said. "That makes you beautiful. I love you."

Mom cried a little. She laughed a little, too. Then she gave me a big hug. "You're beautiful, too," she said. "And I love you very much."

Do you think God thinks Mom and I are both beautiful?

Your beauty should come from within you
— the beauty of a gentle and quiet spirit.
This beauty will never disappear and
it is worth very much to God.

I PETER 3:4

One thing have I desired of the Lord,
that will I seek after; that I may dwell
in the house of the Lord all the days of my life,
to behold the beauty of the Lord.

PSALMS 27:4

Beauty shines
through
In the good that
you do.

You may have meant to hurt me.
But God turned that evil into good.

GENESIS 50:20

Dear God,

Help me to be beautiful by being kind and true and trying hard in every way to speak and act like You.

Help me to see how other people are beautiful too.

Dear God,

You know about that sassy girl at school.

I really wish You would just make her go away.

If You won't do that, please help me be nice to her and show her how much You love her.

Maybe that really is better.

Love the Lord your God.
Love him with all your heart,
all your soul, all your strength,
and all your mind.
Also, you must love your neighbor
as you love yourself.

LUKE 10:27

Dear God,

I love You with all my heart.

But is it ok if I love those pesky kids next door with only half my heart?

Sometimes I know it is the right thing to do and I choose to love them, but my whole heart just doesn't seem to be into it sometimes.

33

THREE LITTLE WORDS

There are three little words
that are so hard to say —
sorry,
forgive,
and obey.

But these three little words
will change your whole day
sorry
forgive,
and obey.

So if you want to be happy
then this is God's way —
tell Him,
"I'm sorry,
please forgive me,
and I'll obey."

Don't forget to say
these three little words
to your parents and others, too.
"I'm sorry,
forgive me,"
Are hard words to say.
But when said from the heart
They bring great joy your way.

A friend loveth at all times.

PROVERBS 17:17

A Friend for Andrew

Andrew had a problem when he was born. Now he can't run as fast as other kids his age. He can't throw a ball as well. He can't jump as high. Actually, Andrew can't do anything like that as well as other kids.

So Andrew is always last when teams are chosen. No one wants him on a team because he helps the team lose. Andrew always feels he isn't as good as them. You know how that feels sometimes, don't you?

Andrew may not throw a ball or jump or run as well as other kids. But he is very smart. He can talk well and is a very friendly boy.

One day a famous NBA star came to
school. He talked with the kids about
basketball. He also talked about loving God
and being a good teammate. "I'm going to
choose one of you to be my guest at my
next game," he said. Of course, the
best basketball players in school
thought it would be them.

But the NBA star walked over
to Andrew. "What's your
name, son?" he asked.

"Andrew," he said.

"I like you, Andrew," said the NBA star. "I want you to be my guest at the next game."

Would it surprise you to know that Andrew became popular in that school? Would it surprise you to know that he became the most popular boy in the whole school?

Do you know someone who needs a special friend? What will you do about it?

Make the one
who's been left out
your special friend.

*Do for other people what
you want them to do for you.*

LUKE 6:31

This is how God showed His love to us:
He sent His only Son into the world
to give us life through Him.

I John 4:9

All creatures
great and small,
The Lord God
loves them all.

Dear God,

Mom says You love all animals because You made them.

Do I have to love skunks and toads just because You do?

Is it ok if I love dogs and cats more?

Do I have to love pesky
kids just because You do?

I guess if You love me,
and You even love pesky
kids, maybe I should love
them, too.

Test everything.
Keep what is good.
And stay away from
everything that is evil.

I Thessalonians 5:21-22

Despise lies.
But be friends
with the truth.

Dear God,

Little lies or big lies make bad friends because they get me in trouble.

But telling the truth helps me know You better.

Your truth is a wonderful friend.

Help me make friends with all Your truths so we can be better friends.

WORDS

Some words are like buckets

that carry lots of things.

Some words are like hornets

that leave some nasty stings.

Some words are like music

that make us want to sing.

Some words are like messengers,

that have good news to bring.

Some words are like hammers,

that beat upon your day.

Some words are like pillows,

that soften what you say.

So when you open up your mouth,

and have some words to share,

Be sure those words are just the words

to really show you care.

A gentle answer
will calm a person's anger.

PROVERBS 15:1

Baseball Cards

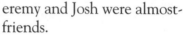

J eremy and Josh were almost-
friends.

They played together but often
didn't have fun together.

They both liked to collect baseball cards.

They just didn't get along together
sometimes.

On Monday, Jeremy and Josh each had
six baseball cards.

But Jeremy stole one card from Josh.

So Jeremy had seven cards and Josh had
five cards.

Josh knew what happened.

So on Tuesday Josh stole two cards from Jeremy.

Now Josh had seven cards and Jeremy had five cards. Jeremy found out.

So on Wednesday Jeremy stole three cards from Josh.

Now Jeremy had eight cards and Josh had four cards.

But Josh learned about this.

So on Thursday Josh stole four cards from Jeremy.

Now Josh had eight cards and Jeremy had four cards. This made Jeremy angry.

So on Friday Jeremy stole five cards from Josh.

Now Josh had three cards and Jeremy had nine cards.

You know how Josh felt.

So on Saturday Josh stole six cards from Jeremy.

But while he was doing that Jeremy stole Josh's three cards.

Now Josh and Jeremy each had six cards. Josh had six cards that he did not have on Monday.

Jeremy had six cards that he did not have on Monday.

So they decided to quit stealing cards.

After all, two wrongs never make a right.

And one wrong each day doesn't make it fun to play!

Two wrongs
never make a right.

*Be sure that no one
pays back wrong for wrong.*

I Thessalonians 5:15

Dear God,

When I give You all my worries and frowns and sin, what do You do with that stuff?

Do You have a big garbage can in heaven? Or do You just make it disappear?

Thanks for never bringing that garbage back to me.

I'm glad You don't recycle it and make me take it back.

Give all your worries to Him,
because He cares for you.

Worry and frowns
Pull the heart down.

*Respect the Lord
and refuse to do wrong.*

PROVERBS 3:7

Dear God,

Someone said that it's like stepping into a dark closet when you do what the devil wants you to do.

You know you're going to fall. You just don't know how far.

And you don't know how much you'll get hurt.

Please God, keep me to always stay away from that closet!

SWING AND SING

All day long

I like to swing.

I swing and sing

A happy song.

When I am sad

I want to swing.

I swing and sing

Until I'm glad.

When things go wrong

I like to swing.

I swing and sing

A Jesus song.

Come, let's sing for joy to the Lord.
Let's shout praises
to the Rock Who saves us.

PSALM 95:1

Sing a song
and
shoo away
sorrows.

Andrew's Dreams

"I had a terrible dream last night," said Andrew. "Monsters were chasing me everywhere."

Mother frowned. "You should have sweet dreams," she said. "Great guys and girls should have great dreams."

"I want to have sweet dreams," said Andrew. "But how can I help what I dream?" "Let's talk about that," said Mother.

"Remember that tv program you begged to see last night. It really was scary, wasn't it?"

Andrew thought for a moment. There were monsters in the tv program. He had even worried about what would happen if those monsters came after him. Andrew knew that the scary tv program may have caused his bad dreams.

"But what should we do?" asked Andrew.

"I'm sorry I let you watch that program," said Mother. "Tonight we'll read about good things and pray before you go to bed."

That night Mother read a wonderful story to Andrew. They talked about God and the wonderful things He does. Then they prayed, and Andrew fell asleep right away.

When he woke up the next morning, Andrew said, "I had good dreams last night. No more scary tv programs before I go to bed."

"Thank You, Lord," said Mother.

"Amen," said Andrew.

Think about the things that are good

and worthy of praise.

PHILIPPIANS 4:8

God did not give us
a spirit that makes us afraid.
He gave us a spirit of power
and love and self-control.

2 TIMOTHY 1:7

Don't fear,
God is near.

I keep trying to reach the goal
and get the prize.

<small>PHILIPPIANS 3:14</small>

Dear God,

You're not afraid of the dark, are You?

Mom says You made the light and the dark, so You can't be afraid of it.

Does that mean You're not afraid of thunder or lightning because You made them, too?

You're really not afraid of
anything, are You, God?

When I'm afraid, I'm going to
ask You to be with me. Then
I won't be afraid. ok, God?

Don't quit or give up,
When struggles you face.
Those who keep trying
Will finish the race.

Dear God,

Help me have a good day.

Help me to smile and do the things I know You want me to do—even when I don't feel like it.

Then, when I go to bed at night, I will be happy.

Thank You for staying with me all day long and helping me.

Whistle in the dark.
Whistle in the day.
Whistle as you work.
Whistle as you pray.

No matter where you are
or the situation there.
Whistle as an act of faith.
Whistle as a prayer!

Dear God,

Is that You whistling when the wind blows?

You're really good, aren't You?

Will You teach me how to whistle Your way?

If You do, I'll whistle a prayer to You. ok?

Never stop praying.

I Thessalonians 5:17

A SMILE IS IN STYLE

A frown runs down,
That's what they say.
A frown is never here to stay.
So if you want a happy day,
A smile
will not
go out
of style.
A grump will slump,
That's what they say.
A grump is never here to stay.
So if you want a happy day,
A smile
will not
go out
of style.

A glare will wear,
That's what they say.
A glare is never here to stay.
So if you want a happy day,
A smile
will not
go out
of style.
A cry goes by,
That's what they say.
A cry is never here to stay.
So if you want a happy day,
A smile
will not
go out
of style.
A pout is out,
That's what they say.

A pout is never here to stay.
So if you want a happy day,
A smile
will not
go out
of style.
A smile is in,
That's what they say.
A smile is always here to stay.
So if you want a happy day,
A smile
will not
go out
of style.
A smile
Never goes out of style.

Be full of joy in the Lord always.

PHILIPPIANS 4:4

Dear God,

I wish I could see You smile and hear You laugh.

Is Your smile something like sunshine?

Is Your laugh something like friendly thunder?

You must smile and laugh a lot at all the funny things people do.

*Happiness
makes a person smile.*

PROVERBS 15:13

Give miles of smiles
in great big piles.

Serve each other with love.

GALATIANS 5:13

Dear God,

I want my hands to be happy hands. So I guess I should do things with them for You and others.

That's better than using my hands just to get stuff to keep, isn't it?

THE WAY TO PRAY

When you pray, do you say now?

If you do, you don't know how.

Do you think that God is late

When He says that you must wait?

Do you think that God is slow

When He really does say no?

Do you thinkthat it is odd

That God is really God?

Do you wonder why it's true

That you are only you?

Do you know that you are blessed

When God gives you what is best?

Remember: when God answers prayer,

His answer may be no, if it's not best for you.

Or it may be wait, not now.

Sometimes we are

asked to wait.

But this we know —

God's never late!

Sometimes we are
asked to wait.
But this we know—
God's never late!

The Lord is good to those
who put their hope in Him.
He is good to those
who look to Him for help.
It is good to wait quietly
for the Lord to save.

LAMENTATIONS 3:25-26

*Do for other people the same things
you want them to do for you.*

MATTHEW 7:12

That Other Girl

mily stood by the door. She looked at the mirror hanging there. Emily saw that other girl, the girl who looked just like her.

Emily waved to the girl. The girl waved back exactly the same way. Emily raised her hand. That other girl raised her hand the same way. When Emily stomped her foot, that other girl stomped right back.

Emily did not like what that other girl was doing. She stuck out her tongue at that other girl, and that other girl stuck out her tongue at Emily. Then Emily made an ugly face at the other girl.

Guess what that other girl did to Emily?

Whatever Emily did, that other girl did to Emily.

Emily yelled at that other girl just as Mother walked into the room.

"Whatever are you doing?" Mother asked.

"Just look at that sassy girl," said Emily. "She's making fun of me. She does everything the same way I do it."

"But that girl is your reflection," said Mother. "She will always do what you do."

"Why doesn't she smile just once?" said Emily.

"She will," said Mother. "But you must smile first."

Emily smiled a little. That other girl smiled a little too.

"She can do better than that," said Mother. "But you must do better than that first."

Emily smiled a big smile. Guess what that other girl did? That's right! She smiled a big smile, too.

"It's the Golden Rule," said Mother. "Do to others as you want them to do to you. Whatever you want others to do, you should first do to them."

So Emily did what mother said.

And that other girl did what Emily did.

Whatever you say,
Whatever you do,
Bounces off others
And comes back to you.

No matter
where you are,
God is
never very far.

God is faithful.
He is the One Who has called you
to share life with His Son,
Jesus Christ our Lord.

I CORINTHIANS 1:9

Dear God,

We had to move again last week. Now I have to find all new friends. I hope I like them.

Dad says we won't have to move anymore when we get to heaven. You'll be there forever and I'll never have to leave my friends because I'm moving.
Wow!

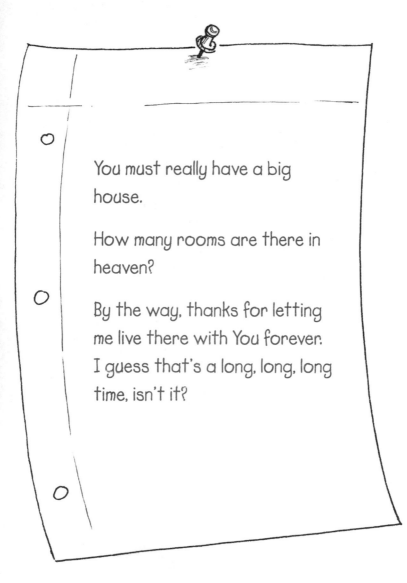

You must really have a big house.

How many rooms are there in heaven?

By the way, thanks for letting me live there with You forever. I guess that's a long, long, long time, isn't it?

Obey now,
Play later.
Disobey now,
Pay later.

If they obey and serve [God],
the rest of their lives will be successful.
And the rest of their years will be happy.
But if they do not listen,
they will die…
without knowing better.

JOB 36:11-12

God has a doorway called yes.
When you walk His ways,
you go through.
But saying NO when
He wants you to go,
Builds a wall in front of you.

My Special Gift

I have a special gift
that I want to give away.
But I know that I can't wrap it
or put it on display.
I'll give it to a person
in a very special way.
I'll give it to my Dad
on this very special day.
So my darling Dad,
this is what I want to say,
My special gift's a special hug
I'll give to you. OK?

Hugs multiply
when you give
them away.

Give, and you will receive.
You will be given much . . . .
The way you give to others
is the way God will give to you.

LUKE 6:38

Don't Lose Hope

"That man who robbed the bank said he had lost hope," said Dad. "He said that's why he robbed the bank." Dad was reading a story in the newspaper.

Amy looked puzzled. "How do you lose hope?" she asked.

Dad thought for a little while. "Do you remember when we hiked in the woods last week?"

Amy frowned. "I got lost," she said.

"We could say that you lost your way," said Dad. "But how did you do that?"

"I got off the path," said Amy.

"You ran off the path when we weren't looking," said Dad. "I had told you to stay on the path with us. I think I even said you could lose your way through the woods filled with trees and shrubs."

Amy smiled. "You did tell me that," she said. "I'm sorry."

"Why didn't you stay on the path?" Dad asked.

"I wanted to chase some squirrels," said Amy.

99

Dad smiled. "You wanted to do what Amy wanted to do," he said. "You didn't trust me when I said you could get lost. But I found you, didn't I?"

Amy gave Dad a hug.

"Losing hope is like losing your way in the woods," said Dad. "As long as you were with me and trusted what I said, you were safe. But when you went your own way, and stopped trusting me to show you the way, you got lost."

"I get it," said Amy. "We lose hope when we stop trusting God to show us the right way."

Dad smiled. "That's it!" he said. "You lose hope, or send it away, when you stop trusting God to lead you in His way."

"I want to keep trusting God," said Amy.

"Then you will not lose hope," said Dad.

Do you think Amy kept trusting God? Will you?

I pray that the God Who gives hope
will fill you with much joy and peace
while you trust in Him.

ROMANS 15:13

*Those who go to
God Most High for safety
will be protected
by God All-Powerful.*

PSALM 91:1

Dear God,

I just heard the story about David and Goliath. Please make me a David and not a Goliath!

Being on Your team means I can face any giant and be a champion—no matter how big I am!

Note: You can read the story of David and Goliath in 1 Samuel, chapter 17.

Faith that does nothing
is worth nothing.

JAMES 2:20

Faith is what you
know is true.
Faith is also
what you do.

Dear God,

I trust You God,
because You're true.

I trust You God,
because You're You!

So help me God,
that I'll be true.

Then You'll trust me,
as I trust You.

SNOWFLAKES AND SUNSETS

Snowflakes,

Sunsets,

Fingerprints,

Family pets.

Each is different.

No two alike.

Just as Mary

Is different from Mike.

God was creative

In what He did.

He made you different
From every other kid.
So aren't you glad,
Whether Luke or Sue,
That in all the world
There is no one like you?
Snowflakes and fingerprints —
You'll always find —
Each one is different, one of a kind.
And just like a snowflake
this, too, is true,
No one else is exactly like you!

Mr. McGrump

Allison wished that Mr. McGrump did not live next door. He looked old. He looked sad. He even looked like his name. Allison thought he looked grumpy.

"I wish someone happy lived next door," Allison said to Mom one day.

"Maybe he's not as sad and grumpy as he looks," said Mom. "Have you ever tried to find out?"

Allison thought about that all day. When she looked in the mirror, she even looked sad and grumpy. "Perhaps he isn't sad or grumpy," said Allison. "I WILL find out. I think that's what Jesus would want me to do." So Allison talked with Mom. "I'm going to visit Mr. McGrump," she said. "I"m going to help him with his chores."

"I think that would be wonderful," said Mom.

Mr. McGrump was certainly surprised to see Allison at the door. "What do you want?" he asked.

"I want to help you do some chores," said Allison. "May I clean your windows for you?"

When Allison finished with the windows she washed some dirty dishes. Then she ran the vacuum cleaner.

Before long Allison was finished. "Time to go home," she said.

"Wait," said Mr. McGrump. "Why did you do that?"

"Because I think Jesus wanted me to do it," she said. "And I don't think you're grumpy at all. I think you're just lonely."

Allison thought she saw a tear coming from Mr. McGrump's eye. Then she knew that she saw two or three tears.

"You're right," he said. "Please come and see me every day. Perhaps you can tell me more about Jesus."

Do you think she did?

Find someone with
a hole in their heart
and fill it with
God's love.

God has poured out His love
to fill our hearts.

ROMANS 5:5

Dear God,

My parents say You can do anything.

Will You dry the dishes for me tonight? Or is that something that I have to do?

I guess if You do Your work, like running the world, I can dry some dishes!

God can do everything!

LUKE 1:37

God is strong and mighty,
creating all things good.
He makes me strong
so I can do the good
I know I should.

*Those people who know they have
great spiritual needs are happy.
The kingdom of heaven belongs to them.*

MATTHEW 5:3

Rely on
God's supply.

Dear God,

Dad says You give us all our food.

You must have a really big kitchen.

Can I see it sometime?

But You won't make me do the dishes, will You?

THANK YOU, GOD

for making my world

so I can live in it,

for giving me food

so I can eat it,

for helping us have a place

so we can live in it,

for giving parents and others

who love me,

so we can do fun things together,

for helping us have God's house

so we can worship You,

for giving me the Bible,

so I can learn about You,

for helping me learn to pray,

so I can talk with You,

and for giving me today,

so I can live for You.

Those who are humble are happy.
The earth will belong to them.

MATTHEW 5:5

A Cheerful Giver

On Saturday Dad gave Jonathan a dollar. "Part of this is for you to spend on anything you want," said Dad. "But you should give part of it to Jesus."

"But how much should I give to Jesus?" Jonathan asked.

"Only what you truly WANT to give," said Dad. "Jesus loves a CHEERFUL giver."

Jonathan began to think about his dollar. "I want to spend it all," he thought. "But I wouldn't feel good about that. So I guess I really do want to give some to Jesus." Jonathan couldn't figure out how much to give to Jesus and how much to spend.

Jonathan thought about the basketball cards he wanted to buy. That made him want to keep all the money. Then he thought about the poor families they talked about in Sunday school last Sunday. That made him want to give it all to Jesus. "I can't spend it all and still give it all to Jesus," he said. "What should I do?"

Then Jonathan had an idea. "I'll give ten cents to Jesus and spend ninety cents on basketball cards," he said.

But Jonathan thought again about the poor people they had talked about in Sunday school. "I guess I'll give ninety cents to Jesus and keep ten cents to spend," he said.

Jonathan didn't feel cheerful about either of these. Next he thought about giving Jesus twenty-five cents and spending seventy-five cents. Or he could give Jesus seventy-five cents and spend twenty-five cents. But Jonathan didn't feel cheerful about either of these. The poor people and the basketball cards were both bouncing around in his mind.

Then Jonathan had another idea. "I know. I'll give Jesus half and spend half," he said. He thought about the basketball cards. He thought about the poor people. The more he thought about giving half and keeping half the more excited he became.

"Well, what did you decide?" Dad asked later.

Jonathan was excited to tell Dad about his decision. He told Dad about how hard it was to make that decision. "You're really a CHEERFUL giver now," said Dad. "I can see that. Now let me tell you what I decided to do. I decided to give you as much as you give Jesus. You can spend that. I decided also to give Jesus as much as you give Him."

Now Jonathan was really excited. He could give Jesus a whole dollar. And he would have a whole dollar to spend. That's what he really wanted to do at first.

"God does love a cheerful giver, doesn't He?" said Jonathan.

You think so too, don't you?

God loves the person
who gives happily.

2 Corinthians 9:7

The Lord is my Shepherd.
I have everything I need.
He gives me rest in green pastures.
He leads me to calm water.
He gives me new strength.

Psalm 23:1-3

Dear God,

Look at that sheep! It has all the grass it can eat. It has a pool of water to drink. And it has a soft, woolly coat to keep it warm. It even has a good shepherd to take care of it. What more could it want?

But do You know what? I have all the food and water I need.

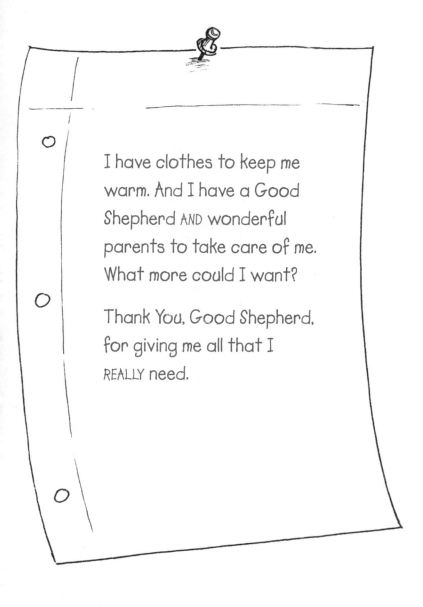

I have clothes to keep me warm. And I have a Good Shepherd AND wonderful parents to take care of me. What more could I want?

Thank You, Good Shepherd, for giving me all that I REALLY need.

*Thanks be to God for His gift
that is too wonderful to explain.*

2 CORINTHIANS 9:15

Count your
many blessings,
Name them
one by one.

Dear God,

I want to count my blessings. But I don't know how to count to a zillion.

Do I have to say "thank you" a zillion times?

LIFE IS A BASKET OF BALLS

Life is a basket of balls
That I toss around each day.

Some are bounced for work,
Others are bounced for play.

When I toss these balls to others,
They toss them back to me.

Sometimes their ball is smaller,
Sometimes it's as big as three.

The balls in the basket are kindness,
And mercy, and joy, and love.

And though each looks like any ball,
They actually came from above.

So when you toss life's balls around
Be careful what you do.

The kind of ball that you may toss
Will always come back to you.

To others be kind, and you will find kindness coming back to you.

Those who give mercy to
others are happy.
Mercy will be given to them.

MATTHEW 5:7

PATIENT, LOVING, AND KIND

When brother's a bother,
a real pesky kid,
be patient, loving, and kind.

When sister is sassy,
at something you did,
be patient, loving, and kind.

When you know something's yours,
and brother says "mine,"
be patient, loving, and kind.

When you want to be quiet
and sis wants to whine,
be patient, loving, and kind.

JUST REMEMBER

When you are a bother,
a real pesky kid,
God's patient, loving, and kind.

When you are sassy
at something God did,
He's patient, loving, and kind.

When you know something's His
but you say "It's mine,"
He's patient, loving, and kind.

When you know you should pray
but you just want to whine,
He's patient, loving, and kind.

Jesus ♥ Me

When brother's a bother
and sister's sassy,
pay them with patience.

Love is patient and kind.

I CORINTHIANS 13:4

It is more blessed to give
than to receive.

ACTS 20:35

Not what you get
But what you give,
Determines the worth
of the life you live.

Dear God,

Do You really get more blessings than You give?

Where do You keep all of them?

You must have a really big blessings box in Your house.

The Father has loved us so much!
He loved us so much
that we are called children of God.

I JOHN 3:1

Dear God,

Mom asked me how I know that she loves me. I told her because she plays and does fun stuff with me.

Then she reminded me that she also washes my clothes and cooks my meals whether I'm good or bad — and that's love too!

Then Mom asked me how did I know that You love me. I replied that You send birds to sing and flowers to smell. Then she reminded me that You also sent Jesus to give His life for me — even before I ever gave my heart to Him! Wow!

Thanks for REALLY loving me.

How Do You Pray?

I know at least a dozen things
That I am looking for.
I'm sure that God has every one,
And maybe even more.
I'd like a sack of money,
A TV set or two.
A VCR would be really neat,
A dozen games would do.
A great big car for Dad to drive,
And maybe one for me.
And if God plans to give us two,
I'm sure He'll give us three.
I know at least a hundred things
That God could send me free.
But God should give them only if
They're really best for me.

We can come to God with no doubts.
This means that when we ask God
for things (and those things agree
with what God wants for us),
then God cares about what we say.

I John 5:14

Love listens.

Trade-in Time

After dinner Dad set up some pieces of cardboard at the kitchen table. "This is the trade-in shop," Dad said. "Bring in today's problems and trade them for something better."

Mom went first. "I've been wearing this frown all afternoon," she said. "I'd like to trade it in for a smile."

Dad drew a picture of a smiling face on a piece of paper and gave it to Mom. It wasn't a very good drawing. In fact, it was so funny that Mom laughed.

"See, it worked," said Dad. "You even got more than you asked for."

Sarah was next. "I said some nasty words to my friend this afternoon," she said. "Can I trade them in?"

"I can't get your nasty words back," said Dad. "But I can give you some new words to give your friend. You can give them to your friend tomorrow."

Dad wrote some words on a piece of paper and gave them to Sarah.

Sarah smiled. Then she read the words to Mom. They said, "I'm sorry. Please forgive me."

"I will give them to her tomorrow," Sarah said. "Maybe she will erase the nasty words I gave her today."

"Now I have a trade-in," said Dad. "Last night you asked me to play a game with you, Sarah. I said I'm too busy. So I'd like to trade those words in for some others." Dad wrote some words on a piece of paper and gave them to Sarah. I LOVE YOU. I'D LIKE TO PLAY A GAME WITH YOU AND MOM.

So they did.

Problems are
opportunities
in disguise.

Those who are sad now are happy.
God will comfort them.

MATTHEW 5:4

If a person is lazy
and doesn't repair the roof,
it will begin to fall.
If he refuses to fix it,
the house will leak.

ECCLESIASTES 10:18

A stitch in time,
saves nine.

Dear God,

Thank You for keeping the world fixed.

You're never too busy to do it. And You're never too lazy either.

But how do You do it?

Do you have a big tool chest?

How big is Your hammer and screwdriver?

Do you use special glue and tape to hold things together?

Whatever You do, thank You for doing it.

147

*Always give thanks to God the Father
for everything.*

EPHESIANS 5:20

It's truly amazing
just what they can do –
Those three little words,
"Please" and "Thank you."

Dear God,

"Please" is like standing outside a door and asking to come in.

"Thank you" is what we say on the other side of the door.

Please, God help me do what You know is best. Thank You, God, for helping me.

Help me remember to say please and thank you to my parents and others, too.

YES, NO, MAYBE SO

Yes, no
Maybe so.
These are words
That you should know.
Please say no
When sin plays rough.
Please say yes
To godly stuff.
Maybe so
Is in between.
You need God's help
To keep you clean.
So please Lord,
Help me know
When to say
Yes, no, and maybe so.

Say no
when you know
That something is wrong.

Say yes
and be blessed
When it's right in God's sight.

*Happy is the person who doesn't listen
to the wicked . . . . He doesn't do what bad people
do. He loves the Lord's teachings. He thinks about
those teachings day and night.*

PSALM 1:1-2

Sharing

GO TEAM

en and Blake were friends. They played together almost every day. Sometimes they had lots of fun playing with and trading their football cards.

One day when they were playing, Ben had five cards and Blake had seven cards.

Blake wanted to share.

So on Monday when Ben and Blake were playing with their football cards, Blake gave Ben one of his football cards. Now Blake had six cards and Ben had six cards. Ben thought about that.

On Tuesday when they were playing, Ben gave Blake two of his football cards.

Now Blake had eight cards. But Ben only had four cards.

Somehow the trading wasn't working out!

So on Wednesday when they were playing, Blake gave Ben three of his cards.

Now Ben had seven cards and Blake only had five cards.

On Thursday when they were playing, Ben gave four of his cards to Blake.

Now Blake had nine cards. Ben only had three cards.

Blake was sure this wasn't fair.

So on Friday when they were playing, Blake gave five of his cards to Ben.

Now Ben had eight cards. Blake had only four cards.

Ben wanted to share with his friend, but things were getting quite confusing!

On Saturday he gave Blake two cards.

Now Blake had six cards and Ben had six cards. Both boys were happy because they had shared.

Finally, both boys had the same number of cards, and they both had some new cards from what they had started with.

"What a neat way to share!" said Blake.

"Cool, isn't it?" said Ben.

What do you think?

Take care
to share.

Do not forget to do good to others.
And share with them what you have.

HEBREWS 13:16

Those who work to bring
peace are happy.
God will call them His sons.

MATTHEW 5:9

Increase
the peace.

Dear God,

What is peace? Is it having less noise? Or is it being happy with lots of noise?

By the way, God, You aren't very noisy are You? I never hear You making lots of noise when You fix the world like Dad does when he fixes things.

How do You do that?

You must REALLY have peace!

You could do good
if you really would.

So if you could, would,
and should,
then why don't
you be good?

Those who are treated badly
for doing good are happy.
The kingdom of heaven belongs to them.

MATTHEW 5:10

NOTHING TO HIDE

When there's nothing to hide
you have peace inside.

When your conscience is clear,
you have nothing to fear.

When your sin's washed away,
you will have a great day.

When you've learned to forgive,
you have learned how to live.

When God cleans your heart,
you will have a new start.

When God's in first place,
you have a joyful face.

When there's
nothing to hide,
You have peace inside.

*If you forgive others
for the things they do wrong,
then your Father in heaven
will also forgive you
for the things you do wrong.*

MATTHEW 6:14

Doing What We Think

"My Sunday school teacher says we do what we think," said Ryan. "Is that true?"

Dad thought for a moment. "Let's check it out," he said.

Dad picked up the newspaper. "Here's a story," he said. "This man robbed a bank. Was he thinking about God or money before he did that?"

Ryan laughed. "That's easy," he said. "Money."

Dad turned the pages. "Here's another story," he said. "A family lost everything when their house burned. But a kind man raised a lot of money to help them. Was he thinking more about this family or himself?"

"The family," said Ryan.

Dad put the newspaper down. "I heard Ryan yell at Jackie yesterday," he said. "Ryan even called Jackie a bad name. Was Ryan thinking about making Jackie happy? Or was Ryan thinking only about what he wanted to do?"

Ryan looked at the floor. He did not know that Dad had heard him.

"I think my Sunday school teacher is right," said Ryan. "We do what we think."

"So what are you thinking now?" asked Dad.

"That I should ask Jackie to forgive me," said Ryan.

Do you think he did what he was thinking?

The thoughts that you think are up to you,

What you think is what you do.

Those who are pure
in their thinking are happy.
They will be with God.

MATTHEW 5:8

Dear God,

My flashlight won't shine because the batteries ran down. Now I can't see where I'm going at night. I can't show my friends which way to go either.

Dad says that's like my Jesus light. When I don't read Your Word, my batteries run down. Then I can't see where You want me to go. And I can't show others where they should go.

Please God, help me keep my Jesus light shining!

In the same way, you should
be a light to other people.
Live so that they will see
the good things you do.
Live so that they will praise
your Father in heaven.

MATTHEW 5:16

Let your light shine.

Dear God,

Thank You for helping me earn that money today.

Please help me know how much to spend, how much to save, and how much to give to Your work.

Please keep me from too much of one and too little of another.

Thank You for showing me Your way.

Wise people store up
the best foods and olive oil.

PROVERBS 21:20

Saving cents
makes sense.

WOULD YOU LIKE
TO BE A DOOR?

Would you like to be a door

That Jesus could go through,

So He could meet all your friends,

As He has first met you?

Would you like to be a window

And let God's light shine through,

So you could help others see

What God has shown to you?

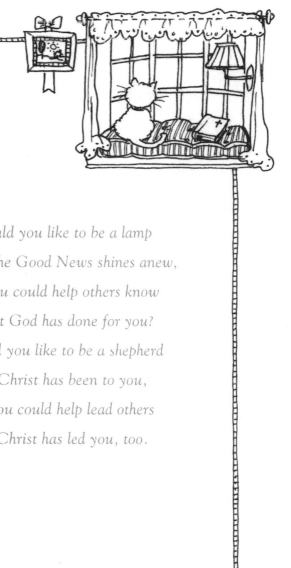

Would you like to be a lamp

Where the Good News shines anew,

So you could help others know

What God has done for you?

Would you like to be a shepherd

As Christ has been to you,

So you could help lead others

As Christ has led you, too.

I stand at the door and knock.
If anyone hears My voice
and opens the door,
I will come in and eat with him.
And he will eat with Me.

REVELATION 3:20

Manners Matter

Eric was playing with his red wagon when Mrs. Minter walked by. She was carrying a big bag of groceries. She looked so tired.

"May I help you?" Eric asked. "You may put your grocery bag in my wagon, and I will pull it home for you." Mrs. Minter lived on the next block.

Mrs. Minter was so glad to put her grocery bag down. She really was tired.

"What a wonderful boy," said Mrs. Minter.

When Eric and Mrs. Minter reached her house, Eric carried her grocery bag into the kitchen.

"I just baked some cookies this morning," said Mrs. Minter. "Would you like one?"

"Please," said Eric.

Mrs. Minter took a cookie from the cookie jar. She gave it to Eric.

"Thank you," said Eric.

"What a polite boy," said Mrs. Minter. When Eric left for home, Mrs. Minter went with him.

Eric's mother was surprised to see Mrs. Minter at the front door with Eric. "Is something the matter?" she asked.

"Yes," said Mrs. Minter. "Manners matter!"

Eric's mother looked puzzled. "Did Eric do something rude?" she asked.

Mrs. Minter laughed. "I don't think Eric COULD do anything rude," she said. "He is the most polite boy I've ever met. I wanted to tell you what a special boy he is." Then Mrs. Minter went home.

Eric's mother smiled. "Manners DO matter," she said to Eric. "You've made four people happy today by showing good manners."

Eric thought for a moment. "I made Mrs. Minter happy," he said. "And I guess I made you happy, too. So that makes me happy. But who is the fourth person?"

"Don't you think Jesus is happy to see all of us happy?" Mother asked.

That really did make Eric happy to think that he made Jesus happy.

"Manners really do matter," said Eric.

You think so too, don't you?

Manners matter.

Love is not rude.

I CORINTHIANS 13:5

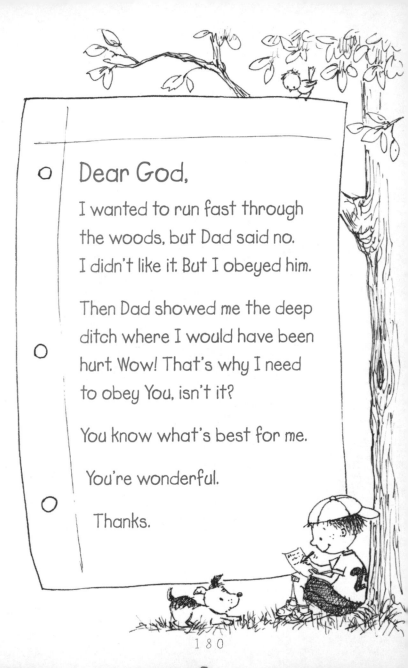

Dear God,

I wanted to run fast through the woods, but Dad said no. I didn't like it. But I obeyed him.

Then Dad showed me the deep ditch where I would have been hurt. Wow! That's why I need to obey You, isn't it?

You know what's best for me.

You're wonderful.

Thanks.

Children, obey your parents
the way the Lord wants.
This is the right thing to do.

EPHESIANS 6:1

*Stand against the devil,
and the devil will run away from you.*

JAMES 4:7

The devil is always
evil behind the "d."

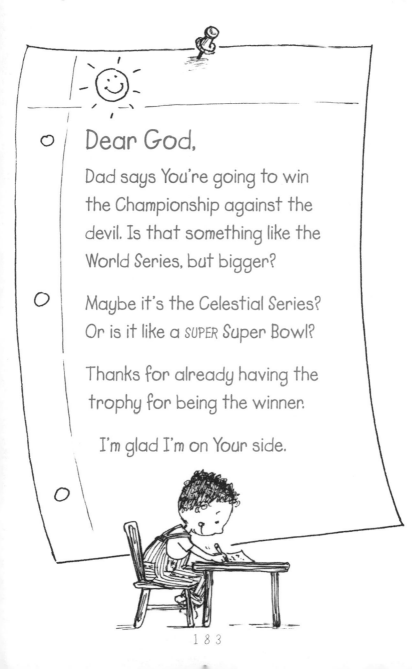

Dear God,

Dad says You're going to win the Championship against the devil. Is that something like the World Series, but bigger?

Maybe it's the Celestial Series? Or is it like a SUPER Super Bowl?

Thanks for already having the trophy for being the winner.

I'm glad I'm on Your side.

WHEN

When I'm scared

or afraid,

Perhaps

I've not prayed.

When my prayers

aren't heard,

Have I forgotten

God's Word?

When I know
I'm not strong,
Perhaps it is that
I've done wrong.

When I want
to do right,
I will walk
in God's light.

When I want
the best day,
I must walk
in His way.

To delight in
the right,
Makes you big
in God's sight.

Those who want to do right
more than anything else are happy.
God will fully satisfy them.

MATTHEW 5:6

"Picker Uppers"

"Jason, you are such a good helper," said Mom. "I love the way you always try to help me."

Jason smiled. He had been feeling sad because his team lost at school. Mom's words were a real "picker upper."

"Thanks, Mom," said Jason. He ran to play with Katy.

Jason and Katy had fun playing together. Today as they were playing, Jason kept thinking about Mom's "picker upper." He had never said something like that to Katy. So he decided to do it now.

"Katy, you are so much fun when we are playing together," said Jason. "I love the way you always make playtime fun."

Katy smiled. She had been feeling sad because no one wanted to sit with her at lunch time at school. Jason's words were a real "picker upper."

"Thanks, Jason," said Katy. When she and Jason finished their playtime, she ran to watch Dad mow the lawn. He was working so hard. As Katy watched, she kept thinking about Jason's "picker upper." She had never said something like that to Dad. So she decided she would do it now.

When Dad stopped for a drink of water Katy gave him a big hug. "Dad, you do so many wonderful things for us," she said. "I love you!"

Dad smiled. He had been feeling sad because his boss had yelled at him at work. Katy's words were a real "picker upper."

"Thanks, Katy," said Dad. He gave Katy a big hug and went into the house. Dad saw Mom hurrying around, getting dinner ready and doing a dozen other little things. Then Dad remembered Katy's "picker upper." He had not said those kinds of things to Mom as much as he should. Dad decided that he would do it now.

Dad walked over and gave Mom a big hug. "Honey, you're wonderful," said Dad. "You do so many great things to help us. Thank you!"

Mom smiled. She had been feeling sad because of some unkind things a friend had said on the phone earlier. Dad's words were a real "picker upper." "Thanks, Honey," she said. Then she called the family to dinner.

You should have seen the smiling faces at the dinner table that night. Do you know why?

Say what people need —
words that will help others
become stronger.

EPHESIANS 4:29

Trust the Lord with all your heart.

PROVERBS 3:5

Trust and obey –
there's no other way!

Dear God,

Mom says You made the world and keep it fixed.

I guess if You can keep the world fixed You can fix my little problems, can't You? I KNOW You can.

Is that what this trust stuff is all about?

Heaven has a party when Jesus is born into a new heart.

Trust in the Lord with all your heart.

PROVERBS 3:5

Dear God,

My Sunday school teacher says
I can start a party in heaven.
All I have to do is help another
kid accept Jesus.

Do You have angel food cake
and heavenly hash ice cream
at Your party?

I really would like to keep
heaven busy with parties.
Help me tell more of my friends
how to accept Jesus. ok?

*Your word is like a
lamp for my feet
and a light for my way.*

PSALM 119:105

Some books
have pictures,
Some make me think,
Some make me laugh,
And some help me cook.
Upstairs, downstairs,
everywhere I look...
The Bible is still
The very best book!

Dear God,

You could have given me a TV program or video to watch. But You gave me a Book to read.

You could have given me a computer game to play. But You gave me a Book called the Bible. You could have given me a Celestial Wide Web to plug into. But You gave me a Book called the Bible.

You must really want me to read Your Book!

I guess I should want to do that, too.

Thank You, God, for Your special Book. Now help me read it.

Also help me know what You want to tell me.

Millions of Yardsticks of Love

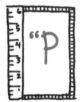

"**P**lease bring the yardstick to me, Kevin," said Mother.

"What's a yardstick?" asked Kevin.

"I'll show you," said Mother. She took the yardstick from the broom closet and showed it to Kevin.

"It's 36 inches long," said Mother. She showed Kevin the numbers on the yardstick. They started with one and went all the way to 36.

"But what do you do with a yardstick?" asked Kevin.

"We measure things," said Mother. "We can measure almost anything with a yardstick."

"Anything?" asked Kevin. "Can it measure love?" Mother smiled. "What kind of love?" she asked.

"Well, I love hot dogs," said Kevin. "How big is that love?"

Mother pointed to number one on the yardstick. "I think it would be about this big," she said. "Maybe it could go to two. But how about your love for your baseball cards. How much would that be?"

Now Kevin smiled. He pointed to number six. "About this much," he said.

Now Mother pointed to number 18. "What do you love this much?" she asked.

"Puppy!" shouted Kevin.

Kevin pointed to number 36, all the way

at the end of the yardstick. "I love you this much," said Kevin.

"And I love you that much too," said Mother. Then Mother gave Kevin a big hug. "But how much do you think God loves you?" Kevin thought for a few moments. "Hundreds and hundreds of yardsticks," he said. "Maybe even millions of yardsticks."

"Would you like to thank God for loving you millions of yardsticks?"

So that's what Kevin did.

For God loved the world so much
that He gave His only Son.
God gave His Son
so that whoever believes
in Him may not be lost,
but have eternal life.

JOHN 3:16

ABOUT
DR. V. GILBERT BEERS . . . .

What kind of a guy would write all this fun stuff? To find out, you'll have to get down on the floor, because that's where he spent a lot of his time with his five kids, and now with his eleven grandkids.

Off the floor he's done some other things, like writing 150 books, mostly for kids, and winning a few awards, like 150 appearances on the bestseller list.

He actually went to school and liked it so well, he stayed and earned two doctor's degrees in communications.

He fell in love with a beautiful princess a long, long time ago, and they have lived happily ever after for 52 years.

Once upon a time, he edited an important magazine called *Christianity Today* and then became president of a company called Scripture Press. Today you'll find him wearing two hats on one head, Vice President of Ministry Development at Cook Communications Ministries, and President of Scripture Press Ministries.

You'd get the impression the guy likes to serve Jesus, wouldn't you?

Additional copies of this book and others in this series are available from your local bookstore.

God's Little Instruction Book for Kids

God's Little Instruction Book for Kids,
  Special Gift Edition

God's Little Devotional Book for Kids

God's Little Instruction Book for Students

God's Little Devotional Book for Students

If you have enjoyed this book,
or if it has impacted your life,
we would like to hear from you.
Please contact us at:

Honor Books
4050 Lee Vance View
Colorado Springs, Colorado 80918

or by e-mail: info@honorbooks.com